I0844057

Bridging Differences

A Human Guide to Cultural Understanding

Table of Contents

Chapter 1. Introduction

In a vibrant and increasingly diverse world, understanding each other becomes both an art and a necessity. Our Special Report, "Bridging Differences: A Human Guide to Cultural Understanding," serves as a heart-warming compass navigating through the fascinating complexities of human diversity. Immerse yourself in engaging worlds as we delve into the heart of various cultures, unravel delightful surprises, and showcase the rewarding experience of mutual understanding. This is not just a report—it's an invitation to embark on an enlightening journey towards unity in diversity from the comfort of your own home. After reading this report, you'll discover that differences aren't barriers, but windows into the intriguing array of human experiences. So, get ready to be captivated, inspired, and surprisingly united, all at the turn of a page!

Chapter 2. Unearthing the Layers: The Anatomy of Culture

Culture is a vast, intricate web that binds people together, attaching them to a shared history, collective understanding, and a unique lens through which they view the world. It is a trove of stories, traditions, and norms that define how a society functions. Let's commence our exploration of this magnificent construct.

2.1. The Concept of Culture

Culture is an umbrella term that encompasses a number of elements including beliefs, values, norms, rituals, symbols, artifacts, and language. These components are interconnected, presenting a unified front that shapes the identity of a group or society.

Cultures are unique; they are developed by the respective societal members over centuries and passed down through generations. They serve as a kind of social glue, uniting individuals under a shared governance of rules, customs, and expectations.

2.2. The Root of Culture: Values

Values are the foundations of a culture. They are deeply ingrained beliefs that guide behavior and decision-making processes. They steer our moral compass and remind us of the acceptable and desirable behaviors within our culture.

The beauty of values lies in their immutable nature. While societal transitions occur, values persist, offering a degree of continuity and stability. They encapsulate the ideals that a culture holds dear, and their preservation is regarded as crucial for the survival of the culture itself.

2.3. Norms and Rituals: The Pillars of Culture

Norms and rituals are the visible aspects of a culture. Norms reflect the 'should' and 'should nots' of a society, while rituals are structured activities that reinforce cultural adherence through repetition.

Norms provide a societal framework, defining the boundaries of behavior. They differ dramatically across cultures, an observation that underscores the importance of understanding the norms of other cultures to avoid misunderstandings and promote harmonious relationships.

Rituals, usually imbued with symbolic significance, are concrete manifestations of deeper cultural values and norms. They add a touch of magic and celebration, giving cultures their unique vibrancy, color, and depth.

2.4. Symbols and Artifacts: Culture's Passport

Symbols represent the abstract concepts of a culture, while artifacts are its tangible expressions. They carry the power to encapsulate cultural values, giving cultures their unique identities.

Both symbols and artifacts hold immense value in understanding a culture. They provide access to a culture's past, shedding light on its evolution and dynamism. They also provide a form of identification, enabling members to belong to a specific cultural group.

2.5. The Power of Language

Language is the lifeblood of culture. It is the bridge that connects individuals, enabling the exchange of cultural components. As the primary medium of communication, language is the vessel that carries a culture's legacy and forms the tapestry of its society.

The symbiotic relationship between language and culture enhances our understanding of both. Each language has its idiosyncrasies that highlight cultural nuances, beliefs, and values.

2.6. The Cultural Shockwave: Acculturation and Assimilation

Cultures are not static; they evolve, influenced by a myriad of factors. One of these factors is interaction with other cultures, leading to the processes of acculturation and assimilation.

Acculturation is a two-way interaction, whereby individuals adapt characteristics of another culture while maintaining aspects of their own. On the other hand, assimilation involves individuals fully integrating into another culture, often at the expense of their original cultural identities.

2.7. The Universal in the Particular: Understanding Cultural Universals

While cultures are unique and diverse, anthropologists argue that certain elements, known as cultural universals, are shared across cultures. These include family values, concepts of morality, art, and language, among others.

Recognizing cultural universals can facilitate a sense of shared humanity among diverse cultures. It is these shared facets of human life that act as a reminder of our shared human existence, encouraging empathy and understanding.

Drawn in from the expansive canvas of culture, these slices of information help us comprehend the sheer depth and breadth of what culture entails. By looking under the skin of societies, we can not only appreciate the diversity that exists but also the threads of commonality that weave us together into a shared human narrative. The anatomy of culture, as complex as this dissection has shown it to be, is equally wondrous and invites our continued endeavours to learn, understand, and celebrate.

As this chapter frames the contours of culture's anatomy, the forthcoming chapters will dive deeper into specific cultures, allowing you to traverse the dynamic landscape of human cultural diversity. Prepare yourself to embark on a journey of understanding, empathy, and rich diversity as we delve deeper.

Chapter 3. Celebrating Human Diversity: A World of Difference

In a world that stretches from the deserts of the Sahara to the icy landscapes of Antarctica, the diversity of humanity is beyond staggering. Every corner of the planet is teaming with vibrant cultures, thousands of languages, and innumerable traditions. Our differences make us who we are. However, to truly appreciate this melange, we must step into the worlds of others, understand their customs, perceive their view of life, and find common ground not despite, but through these differences. This is how we truly celebrate human diversity.

3.1. The Many Ingredients of Human Diversity

Diversity in humans is not just restricted to physical differences but extends into the realms of language, religion, traditions, lifestyles, and countless other aspects. Each element of culture shapes the members of a community, forming unique identities that make every group of humans distinct from another.

Language, for instance, is not just about communication. It is the vessel that carries a culture's folklore, history, and worldview. It is deeply intertwined with how members of a culture think and perceive reality. The diversity of languages, over 7000, each with its distinct phonetics and grammar, is a testament to the multifaceted nature of human minds.

Religion and spiritual beliefs, too, provide an intimate view into a culture's psyche. They reveal how a culture understands life, death, morality, and the universe. Whether it's the polytheistic beliefs of Hindus, monotheism of Christianity, Islam and Judaism, or the animism practiced by many indigenous cultures, each spiritual system provides a distinct, profound perspective on existential questions.

3.2. The Benefits of Embracing Diversity

In spite of the conflicts and misunderstandings diversity can sometimes create, it's worth remembering that diversity also produces great benefits. The first and most obvious is innovation. When diverse minds converge, they bring unique perspectives to the table. The intersection of varied ideas fosters creative solutions, new ways of thinking, and groundbreaking innovations.

Diversity also fosters learning and growth. When we strive to understand cultures different from ours, we not only gain fascinating insights but also shatter our preconceived notions. This process aids in cognitive flexibility, critical thinking, and emotional intelligence, which are pivotal for personal and societal development.

Further, diversity is essential for sustainability. Various cultures have adapted to their environments in different ways, developing unique sustainable practices. For instance, traditional societies in arid regions have perfected water conservation methods, while certain tribes have techniques to preserve biodiversity. Learning from these cultures could provide key solutions to our ongoing environmental challenges.

3.3. Overcoming the Barriers of Cultural Understanding

Cultural understanding doesn't come easily. It's often easier to stick to what we know and adhere to the conventions of our own culture. However, moving past stereotypes, practicing genuine curiosity, demonstrating empathy, and cultivating open-mindedness can help bridge cultural differences.

Stereotypes are oversimplified perceptions we have about a group which can often be misleading or utterly false. They create invisible walls and prevent meaningful understanding. Overcoming stereotypes requires conscious effort to seek accurate information and form more nuanced perceptions.

Curiosity propels us towards understanding. It encourages us to question, explore, and delve deeply into unfamiliar cultures. Curiosity paves the path to knowledge and tolerance. Displaying genuine interest in learning about other cultures creates positive exchanges and shared understanding.

Empathy helps us to emotionally resonate with others, to feel what they're feeling, and to understand their perspectives. It enables us to see the world from their eyes, fostering a human connection extending beyond cultural lines. Empathy, however, needs practice - it requires us to be patient, attentive, and truly open to experiencing the emotions of others.

Understanding diversity is not an overnight task, nor is it a destination. It's a continuous process, an ongoing journey of exploration, learning, and connection. In this globalized world, it's become an essential endeavour not only for personal growth but also for fostering peaceful co-existence. As we begin to understand and appreciate our differences, we realize that they are not barriers, but opportunities for learning, discovery, and mutual enrichment. After all, it is our array of differences that shapes the beautiful mosaic of humanity.

Chapter 4. Traditions: Honoring the Past, Shaping the Present

In the rich tapestry of human experience, traditions act as the resilient threads holding communities together. They offer a unique vantage point from which we can glimpse into the essence of various cultures; a time-honored bridge connecting the past to the present, shaping identities and molding societies. Let's dive deep into this fascinating world.

4.1. Understanding Traditions

To grasp the significance of traditions, we must first understand what they are. Our tale begins in the distant past when human communities started forming. As societies evolved and cultures developed, certain behaviors, practices, and beliefs emerged that each grouping regarded as essential. Over centuries, these practices and beliefs were passed down generations, becoming "traditional."

Traditions can be seen in varied aspects of life, from simple daily routines to grandeur community events—from the serene Japanese tea ceremonies to the spirited samba parades of Brazil. While appearing diverse, each tradition stems from a shared history, reflects a communal spirit, and inspires a collective identity.

4.2. The Role of Traditions

Deeply woven into every facet of human life, traditions perform manifold roles.

They transmit culture and knowledge down the generations,

fostering continuity and consistency. Take the age-old Maori tradition of passing down legends, myths, and history through carefully structured narratives, effectively ensuring the survival of their rich cultural heritage even in modern times.

Traditions also bestow individual identity and a sense of belonging. For instance, the bar and bat mitzvahs in Jewish culture are key rites of passage, marking the transition from childhood to adulthood.

Additionally, traditions serve as tools for social cohesion, fostering a sense of unity and collective decision-making, as seen in the indigenous tribal councils present in various cultures worldwide.

4.3. Ceremonies and Celebrations

A vibrant aspect of culture lies in its ceremonies and celebrations. They are visceral displays of tradition, the community's heartbeat resonating with the rhythm of the past- present continuum.

For instance, the Chinese New Year, with its innumerable customs, illuminates China's cultural essence. The sweeping cleanliness drive symbolizes the sweeping away of ill-fortune, the lanterns light the way for the Lunar New Year, while the dragons and fireworks ward off evil spirits. Intricate in its rituals, yet universal in its themes of renewal, unity, and fortune, it is a testament to the strength of tradition.

Diwali, the Festival of Lights in India, exemplifies traditions molding society. Massive light displays represent the victory of light over darkness, knowledge over ignorance, and herald prosperity. Here, tradition serves as an identifier uniting the diverse Indian population with a shared story.

4.4. The Cultural Value of Cuisine

Food is perhaps one of the most delicious expressions of tradition. Each regional cuisine carries stories from the past, evolving tastes of the present, and a legacy for future generations. The meticulous Japanese sushi preparation highlights the importance they place on precision and aesthetic. Meanwhile, the communal cooking and feasting during American Thanksgiving symbolize gratitude and togetherness.

4.5. Traditions in Crisis and Resilience

Traditions, much like the cultures they embody, are not static. They adjust, adapt, and painfully at times, risk being lost. Modernization, migration, and globalization pose challenges. Despite this, traditions show remarkable resilience.

The Polynesians, despite dwindled traditional navigation knowledge, initiated the Polynesian Voyaging Society to revive their seafaring heritage. This cultural renaissance showcases how traditions can reemerge even when they seem to border on oblivion.

4.6. Traditions: A Journey, Not A Destination

Remember, traditions are not relics to be merely venerated; they are living extensions of a community's spirit - breathing, evolving, and growing. Our exploration of traditions aims to nudge readers towards appreciating this dynamic aspect of culture, understanding its complex roles, and absorbing its humane lessons.

In understanding and honoring traditions, we stand to gain insight into the rich diversity of human experiences. We uncover a shared heritage of wisdom, resilience, and continuity that transcends boundaries and time. And we grasp, with profound respect, the beautiful fact that while traditions shape us, we also shape traditions in the vibrant symphony of cultural evolution.

Chapter 5. Languages: The Heartbeat of Cultural Identity

Beginnings of Language ===

In the birth of civilizations, language emerged as a tool to foster communication and connection. Every word woven into the tapestry of our societal fabric reveals a rich tapestry of human history and cultural nuance. Language, in its essence, is much more than a mere tool for communication. It is a heartbeat — the vibrant pulse of cultural identity.

Across the globe, approximately 7,000 languages bring millions of people together. Languages with lyrical nuances, silent letters, and fascinating scripts. Languages that have journeyed from ancient carvings on the walls of a hidden cave to the digital lines of code making up the modern internet. Understanding these languages deepens our appreciation of culture and its many vibrant shades.

5.1. Language and Cultural Identity

The relationship between language and cultural identity is profound. Language acts as the transporter of culture, carrying cultural norms, values, and historical narratives from one generation to another. It mirrors the philosophies, social structures, and even the geographical locales of the culture it represents, thereby helping to construct and uphold a society's cultural identity.

A speaker of Japanese, for instance, might explain the concept of "Omotenashi" — a word encapsulating warm hospitality that anticipates a guest's needs. Or take Germany, where "Waldeinsamkeit" — a feeling of solitude, being alone in the woods and a connectedness to nature, reflects a deep-rooted cultural identity linked to nature.

Every language, with its idioms and phrases, encapsulates the past, defines the present, and shapes the future of its people, helping each individual to identify and connect with their respective cultures.

5.2. Language Diversity: A Melting Pot of Cultures

Language diversity is one of the world's greatest strengths; it highlights the immense spectrum of human thought, philosophy, and expression. Consider Papua New Guinea, a country smaller than Spain in size, but astonishingly rich in linguistic variety where over 800 languages are spoken.

Africa, the cradle of humankind, boasts some 2,000 languages, weaving a giant mosaic of culture. In Europe, while English, French, and German are widespread, hundreds of regional languages like Basque, Catalan, and Sami remain key cultural identifiers.

The beauty of human experience lies in its endless variation, and the vast array of languages worldwide serves to highlight this critical aspect of humanity.

5.3. The Influence of Language on Thought

The connection between language and thought, often referred to as the Sapir-Whorf hypothesis, posits that language actively shapes or influences our thought processes. The diversity of languages leads to diversity in thought and perception.

For example, in languages like Hopi, an Uto-Aztecan language of

North America, there is no concept of time as understood in many other languages, which effects their perception of time and thus reality. Similarly, the Australian Aboriginal Guugu Yimithirr only uses cardinal directions (north, south, east, and west) instead of egocentric coordinates (left, right, front and back), which results in an inherently different spatial cognition.

Hence, language and thought are intertwined in a dynamic dance. A step in the direction of understanding a new language is a step in broadening one's cognitive horizon, seeing the world from an entirely different perspective.

5.4. Language Evolution and Cultural Adaptation

Languages, like the cultures they mirror, aren't static; instead, they are living, breathing entities that evolve with time. This evolution of language is tied closely to cultural adaptation. When cultures interact, languages morph and adapt, taking on new words, phrases, and constructs.

The rise of internet and the fast-paced world it ushered in gave birth to new languages like coding languages, and molded modern lexicons with words like 'selfie', 'meme', and 'troll'. Sometimes, however, when new languages form, older ones fade away, taking with them a wealth of cultural wealth, a phenomenon known as language extinction.

Retaining linguistic diversity is therefore essential. Each language that is kept alive is a testament to the dynamic nature of human intellect and skills, whose loss would diminish our understanding of human history and cultural diversity.

5.5. The Art of Language Learning

Language learning isn't only a cognitive exercise, it is an immersion into a new cultural identity. Deciphering a language's idioms, phrases, and even its grammatical rules offers a fascinating understanding of its corresponding culture. To learn the Aboriginal Yolngu concept of 'Djarrma', one learns to appreciate the inherent value of balance and harmony in the cosmos of this indigenous Australian culture.

In conclusion, language is a vibrant embodiment of cultural identity. It enriches our comprehension of the depth, beauty and diversity existing within human cultures. Understanding and preserving this linguistic diversity is an acknowledgement of our shared humanity, for in every language we hear echoes of our collective journey - a resounding story of human ingenuity and adaptability.

Chapter 6. Religion and Beliefs: The Soul of a Culture

The myriad tapestry of human belief systems is as diverse as it is profound. From age-old religious practices to contemporary spiritual ideas, they serve as a looking glass into the very essence of peoples and cultures around the globe. Navigating through these myriad belief systems, we'll begin to appreciate their key elements, symbols, shared values, and unique nuances. As we journey through the labyrinth of this chapter, we discover that the core of each belief system resonates with invaluable lessons about human life, wisdom, and the collective past.

6.1. The Threading of Time and Beliefs

Religious and spiritual beliefs are deeply intertwined with the progression of time. They evolve, just as societies do, with each epoch offering its unique flavors and influencing the interpretation and practice of these beliefs.

The ancient societies of Mesopotamia, for instance, nourished some of the first known spiritual systems. Forming a complex polytheistic mash, they believed in a divine assembly overseeing various aspects of existence. These deities, often tied with natural phenomena, governed their lives in every perceivable dimension. Similarly, ancient Egypt's polytheistic practice reverberated with beliefs in an afterlife, evident in their elaborate traditions associated with death and burial.

The Axial Age, spanning 800 BCE to 300 BCE, witnessed the sea-change from polytheism to the emergence of monotheistic doctrines, as seen in the birth of Judaism, Buddhism, Confucianism, and in the philosophies of ancient Greece. It also marked the transformation of Hinduism, capturing its grand epics and philosophical Upanishads that delved into metaphysical questions about the self and the universe.

The Common Era saw the rise of monotheistic religions, notably Christianity and Islam, each bringing a new perspective of divinity while also establishing codes for moral and ethical living. Other systems of belief, such as the Dharmic religions of the East evolved in parallel, fostering paths like Buddhism, Jainism, and Sikhism.

In more recent times, society has seen a combination of secularization and a surge in new religions and spiritual movements, many of them founded on individual experience rather than traditional doctrines. This melange reflects our continued quest for spiritual fulfillment and moral guidance.

6.2. Symbols and Rituals: Mirrors of Beliefs

Understanding the symbols and rituals associated with each religion is akin to deciphering a complex and abstract language – a language of metaphors and deep-seated meanings that bridge the gap between the sacred and the human.

Symbols like the Cross for Christianity, the Star of David for Judaism, or the Om symbol in Hinduism are not just logos using visual language. They represent an entire belief system, rich in historical, cultural, theological, and cosmic significance. Similarly, rituals, whether it's the Muslim's obligatory prayer (Salat) five times a day, the Christian Eucharist, or the Hindu Puja, express an intricate pattern of religious life.

Rites of passage in almost every faith tradition – Baptism in Christianity, Bar Mitzvah in Judaism, the 'Upanayana' (thread ceremony) in Hinduism – symbolize the transition of an individual from one stage of life to another, binding believers together in a shared sense of time and space.

6.3. The Shared Values Betwixt

Despite the stark diversity in belief systems, there are shared values that most, if not all, espouse. Respect for elders, hospitality, cherishing life, community service, and the golden rule of treating others as you would like to be treated echo across cultures, binding humanity together beyond the fringes of individual faiths.

Even as we relish this unity, it's equally important to appreciate the diversities that give each faith its unique charm. Thus, lie the harmonious balance and the challenges of cultural understanding – to concurrently appreciate the unity and uniqueness of each faith tradition.

6.4. Nuances: Beliefs Within Beliefs

To delve deeper requires recognizing the nuances within each faith itself. There is no single Christianity, Islam, Buddhism, Hinduism, or any other religion, but rather a myriad of interpretations, denominations, sects, and practices within each. For instance, Sunni and Shia in Islam, Protestant and Catholic in Christianity, Theravada and Mahayana in Buddhism, denote more than simple subdivisions; they represent distinct expressions of faith and worldviews.

Even within these subdivisions, individual experiences and interpretations shape religious practice, turning it into a deeply personal, fluid journey. This intricate weave gives each culture its distinct spiritual vibe, reflecting its history, its philosophy, and its spirit.

As we conclude our foray into the realm of religion and beliefs, we grasp how these systems form an integral part of our cultural identity. They shape our worldview, influence our ethics, and instill a sense of purpose. Above all, they narrate the story of humankind through the ages, preserving our collective wisdom, our struggles, victories, hopes, and aspirations. Understanding this vast spectrum of belief systems may be complex, yet it is a journey worth traversing in our shared endeavor to sow the seeds of unity amid diversity. The diversity of religious beliefs is not a wall segregating us but a spectrum of vibrant colors, painting the beautiful picture that is humankind.

Chapter 7. The Flavors of Culture: Exploring Global Culinary Delights

Food is an expression of culture—an edible exploration into a place, its people, and their traditions. Around the world, dishes tell unique stories that reflect local methods, ingredients, customs, and histories. Within the cornucopia of edible tradition and culinary creativity, there's an intriguing array of tastes, fragrances, textures, and experiences awaiting the curious palate. Join us on this culinary voyage as we explore the beautiful tapestry of global gastronomy.

7.1. The Spice Routes: Remnants of the Age of Exploration

Our gastronomic sojourn starts with the thrilling tales of ancient trade routes. Known for their key role in linking the East and the West, these trade routes paved the way for the introduction of a wide assortment of spices to different cuisines. Nutmeg and cloves from the Indonesian Spice Islands, pepper and cardamom from India, and cinnamon from Sri Lanka flooded the global market.

Back then, these spices weren't just culinary game-changers; they were symbols of wealth and power. A merchant with a chest full of these exotic goods could afford anything their heart desired. It was the commercial demand for these spices that fueled explorations and led to contact, conflict, eventual cultural exchange and fusion of culinary traditions.

These days, spices continue to inject life into the world's pots and pans. From the warm notes of cinnamon in a Mexican hot chocolate to the fiery heat of the Indian curry, these fragrant tokens of the past continue to tickle our senses and enrich our dining experiences.

7.2. Soup, an Intimate Expression of Culture

The next stop on our culinary tour is a certain dish that features across cultures—the soup. Serving as a culinary language that transcends borders, soups brim with significant insights about the places from which they hail.

Consider Vietnam, where a bowl of pho keeps the culinary spirit alive. This deceptively simple soup narrates a tale of resilience, combining influences from Vietnam's colonial past and ingredients sourced from its rich soils. Or consider the hearty textures of Ukrainian Borsch—a stew filled with meat and vegetables, reflecting the country's agrarian roots.

7.3. The Ceremony of Eating: More Than Food

Now that we've whetted our appetite, let's set the table and explore the rituals and ceremonies that encapsulate the act of eating. The act of consuming food is not just about sustenance—it's a communal experience steeped in long-standing tradition and respect for food.

Take Japan, for instance. Here, the tea ceremony—Chado, or "The Way of Tea"—captures Zen principles. Meanwhile, in Ethiopia, the coffee ceremony, Bunna, is not just about enjoying a cup of java—it's an integral part of their social and cultural fabric. From using the "jebena" (clay pot) to roasting, grinding, and brewing the coffee beans, each step has a meaning, bringing people together in a moment of community and reverence for tradition.

In another corner of the world, in Spain, people engage in

"sobremesa"—a time spent lingering at the table after the meal, savoring conversation and company. The act of eating extends beyond the last bite, highlighting the integral role of communication and companionship in the human eating experience.

7.4. The Art of Bread: Grain, Water, and Culture

Ask about staple foods, and in most parts of the world, you'll hear about bread. Bread is the ultimate product of agricultural success, a testament to the human ability to shape their environment and manipulate the world's elements into a desirable outcome.

As we bite into a piece of bread, we're experiencing a slice of cultural history. The crusty baguette of France, the fluffy naan from India, the pita bread of the Middle-East or the dense rye loaves of Russia—all of these are much more than a side dish. They are emblems of identity, a talking point at the dining table, a catalyst for social interaction, and a symbol of hospitality.

7.5. The Sweet Finish: Desserts and Their Cultural Significance

No culinary journey is complete without a detour into the realm of sweetness—desserts. Much like main course dishes, desserts also mirror the diversities of cultures across the globe.

For instance, Baklava—a honey-soaked, nut-filled pastry conjures tales of the legendary Ottoman Empire, while the French Macaron encapsulates precision, elegance, and a subtle indulgence, mirroring the keynotes of French culture. The Tres-Leches cake from Latin America, drenched in three kinds of milk, expresses joy and celebration. India's vast repertoire of confections, like "Gulab Jamun" or "Jalebi," bespeaks of the country's sweetness and love for vibrant celebrations.

Food is never merely food—it is a testament to human history, shared experiences, celebration, sustenance, and cultural evolution. The act of learning about, preparing, sharing, and relishing food is invariably an act of understanding humanity. As we close this chapter, we hope that this journey left your intellectual palate well-travelled and your spirits, like a well-simmered stew, richly infused with knowledge of our vibrant world. As we progress to unearthing more human experiences in the subsequent chapters, may we continue to understand that, though the flavors of culture may be diverse, there is a unity in our shared experiences.

Chapter 8. Societal Structures: Diverse Frameworks of Living Together

People live together in varied societal formations. Within these formations is a rich tapestry of human experience, shaped by an array of cultural, environmental, religious, and political influences. These societal structures often govern aspects of daily life, from the large-scale like government and division of labor, to the more intimate, such as family life, friendship groups, and community building.

Let's embark on a vibrant exploration, dissecting the intricate framework of societal structures around the globe.

8.1. The Tapestry of Family Structures

Nuclear and extended families provide the first societal structure most of us encounter. Varied in form and function, these are influenced by factors like geographical location, cultural practices, and societal norms.

In Western societies, the nuclear family – consisting of parents and their offspring – dominates. However, we witness changes with the advent of blended families, same-sex family units, and shared custody arrangements.

Contrastingly, collectivist cultures, such as in Asia and Africa, emphasize extended family living. These include grandparents, uncles, aunts, and cousins under one roof, or very nearby. Community comes first, and the family unit tends to be geared towards the collective good, rather than individual accomplishments.

8.2. Societal Hierarchies and Shared Responsibility

Societal structure isn't only about familial relationships. It also pertains to how roles and responsibilities get divided. Distinctive societal hierarchies come with their own set of shared responsibilities and governance.

Feudal systems once emphasized hierarchical relationships, with clear demarcations of power between monarchs, lords, vassals, and serfs, often within a single geographical domain.

On the other hand, indigenous societies have aimed for more egalitarian structures. For instance, the Iroquois Confederacy of North America set up a sophisticated democratic system, where decisions were based on consensus.

In the nomadic Tuareg society in the Sahara, roles are inversely divided with the "maternalistic" structure, where women dictate the societal hierarchy.

8.3. Community Cohesion and Celebration

Critical to many societies is the fostering of community bonds—be it through shared work, ceremonies, or celebrations.

Festivals and traditional celebrations are crucial in communities worldwide, reinforcing shared cultural values, offering a communal respite from labor, or marking significant life events.

In India's agrarian society, the festival of Pongal celebrates the auspicious harvest season, rewarding the year's hard work. Similarly, American Thanksgiving traces its roots back to the harvest festival.

Shared happenings like these act as societal glue, binding people together and reinforcing a sense of communal kinship.

8.4. Education and the Facilitation of Learning

Education structures differ remarkably worldwide. Western societies typically utilize a formal, grading system-oriented education.

However, informal education prevails in other cultures. For instance, Maasai children in East Africa often observe and emulate adults, acquiring practical skills essential for their pastoral lifestyle.

Online learning, homeschooling, and unschooling are recent disruptive educational structures, demonstrating adaptiveness to changing societal needs.

8.5. Matrimony and Partnering Patterns

Matrimony patterns keep societies evolving, marking significant aspects of societal order.

Monogamy, multiple partners, arranged matches, and love marriages each have a unique place. For instance, in Tibet's polyandric society, a woman typically marries all the brothers in a family to prevent division of land.

In societies valuing individualistic goal attainment, like the U.S., individuals often delay marriage to pursue education or career first.

8.6. Towards Understanding Our Shared Humanity

Diverse societal structures offer windows into the multifaceted human experience, reminding us how culture and customs shape our lives while celebrating our shared humanity. Broadening our understanding of these frameworks arms us with insight and empathy, rewarding not just our intellect but our hearts, as well.

Appreciating diversity thus illuminates the unifying threads stitched into the rich fabric of human cultures. In this enlightened understanding, we might find that the world—despite its spectacular variety—is a village after all, bound by shared human values and aspirations.

Chapter 9. Artistic Expressions: Culture's Vibrant Storytellers

Any discourse on culture is incomplete without diving into the vibrant world of artistic expressions—an expansive realm that allows the color, ethos, history, and heart of a civilization to be eloquently unveiled. Art, in its multitude of forms, transcends language barriers and geographical boundaries. It delivers profound messages, opens doors to new perspectives, and serves as powerful storytellers of cultural narratives.

9.1. The Brushstroke of Identity

The canvas of visual arts has often been the first point of reference to understand cultural nuances. From the delicate calligraphy of Eastern calligraphers to the rich tapestries of the Medieval Europe, and the intricate Madhubani paintings of India to the daring strokes of African tribal art—the variety is both staggering and revealing. Each brushstroke, be it on rice paper, cave walls, or parchments, illuminates the identity of its people—their beliefs, their successes, their struggles, and their evolution over time.

Examining the Aboriginal art of Australia, for example, acquaints us with the dreamtime stories and spiritual beliefs of the indigenous population. The art, characterized by intricate dot patterns and animal forms, is not only aesthetically pleasing, but also a repository of ancient wisdom, offering insights into the oldest continuous culture on the planet.

9.2. Choreographed Histories: The Dance of Culture

Dance, another pillar of artistic expression, is a dynamic reflection of the people's relationship with their natural, spiritual, and social surroundings. The vigorous leaps of the Maasai warriors in Kenya, for example, are not merely an athletic feat but an assertion of their resilience and martial prowess. On the other hand, the delicate pirouettes of ballet mirror the grace and formality of European court cultures.

Contrastingly, the energetic samba rhythms of Brazil born from the mixture of African, Portuguese and native traditions, reveal a culture that embraces joy, sensuality, and communal celebration. Dance, thus, is more than a performance—it's a living, breathing chronicle of histories and experiences, a silent yet poignant communicator.

9.3. The Resonance of Belonging: Culture through Music

Like dance, music is a universal language that weaves together the threads of cultural identity and collective memory. The melancholic strains of the Portuguese Fado speaks volumes of saudade—a deep, untranslatable yearning. Tuareg musicians from the Sahara Desert, with their compelling desert blues, voice the nomadic people's yearning for freedom against political unrest. The lively Polka tunes, on the other hand, sing of Central European camaraderie and festive spirits.

The haunting Australian didgeridoo, the soothing Japanese koto, the spirited African djembe—each instrument, each melody, conveys stories and emotions that textbooks often overlook.

9.4. Word Weavers: Literature as the Mirror of Culture

Literature, undoubtedly, offers the deepest and most detailed glimpse into cultural landscapes. Be it the heroic sagas of the Norsemen, the lyrical poetry of Persian Sufis, the stark realism of Russian novelists or the powerful oratory of Native American leaders—every tale, every metaphor, every dialogue leads us towards a better understanding of the people it stems from.

Meticulous reading of Gabriel García Márquez's works uncovers the realities of South America, marred by civil unrest, yet brimming with magical realism. Similarly, African literature—rich with oral tradition, proverbs, and folklore—takes us on a journey through communal living, ancestral wisdom, and the complex web of colonialism and post-colonial identity.

9.5. Enigmatic Narratives: The Art of Storytelling

Oral storytelling traditions, too, deserve acknowledgment. They have long been the medium through which generational wisdom, heroic feats, divine interactions and moral codes have been passed down. For instance, the griots of West Africa, the seanachaís of Ireland, or the aborigines of Australia hold a special place in societal structures with their unique storytelling styles.

Thus, artistic expressions carry the heartbeats of the cultures they belong to. They invite us on an immersive journey, allowing us to understand diverse civilizations not merely in terms of dates and events but as complex human societies molded by beliefs, values, hopes, struggles, and dreams. By exploring art, dance, music, literature, and storytelling, we uncover the spectrums of cultural realities, finding commonalities amid differences, and celebrating the human spirit's vibrancy. The world becomes a familiar place, and as the curtain falls, we stand united—not despite, but because of our diversity.

Chapter 10. Overcoming Cultural Misunderstandings: Keys to Dialogues

Human interaction is a dance of nuances, gestures, and unsaid words. It's a choreography conducted by recognisable cultural patterns. As we endeavor to comprehend these patterns, we occasionally misstep. It is the humility to rise again and the resilience to place one careful foot in front of the other that fuels our journey towards cultural understanding—let's unpack this process.

10.1. Understanding Cultural Misunderstandings

Cultural misunderstandings stem from the disparity in attitudes, values, or manners that often go unobserved during intercultural interactions. The disparities can lead to confusion, conflict or discomfort, which creates a barrier in communication. These misunderstandings can occur within an individual, like internalizing stereotypes, or at a societal level, like accepting the status quo without questioning.

There is also a concept known as 'culture shock,' where an individual experiences unease, anxiety, or disorientation upon exposure to a new cultural setting. Being subjected to new languages, behaviors, norms, and expectations can cause an individual to feel isolated and overwhelmed. These experiences highlight the significance of facilitating cultural understanding and the consequences of neglecting it.

10.2. The Role of Stereotypes and Bias

Stereotypes are generalized, oversimplified views of people, often based on their group affiliations—whether nationality, religion, or race. These beliefs, while not always negative, are rarely an accurate representation of the individual or group in question. They can act as barriers to effective intercultural dialogues, leading to misconceptions and cultural misunderstandings.

Similarly, bias plays a substantial role in shaping our perceptions. Bias can be so deeply ingrained that individuals hardly recognize its presence or influence. Unconscious bias can lead to stereotyping, discrimination, and generalized assumptions which further intensify cultural misunderstandings. Recognizing these biases is the first step toward overcoming them.

10.3. Tools for Cultural Understanding

10.3.1. Communication

Clear and explicit communication is an essential tool for cultural understanding. Being articulate, considerate, and open-minded can promote effective dialogue. Using 'I' statements can reflect a personal viewpoint without generalizing or offending others. Regularly reflecting on our conversation can also help us detect and rectify any miscommunications.

Embracing patience can ensure that everyone feels heard and respected. Slowing down to appreciate the tempo of our dialogue can make room for empathy and understanding.

10.3.2. Active Listening

Active listening involves reflecting on what the speaker is saying, how they're saying it, and what they might be leaving unsaid. It requires us to set aside our own thoughts and feelings to truly engage with the speaker on their own terms, without passing judgments or trying to 'solve' their problems.

Active listening fosters a supportive, cooperative, and respectful environment where ideas are exchanged, and perspectives are broadened.

10.3.3. Empathy

Building empathy can foster more constructive dialogues, bolstering effective communication. With empathy, we not only understand the experiences and feelings of the speaker, but also connect with them on a shared emotional level.

Empathy helps us to transcend our confined perspectives, opening us up to new ideas, experiences, and ways of perceiving the world.

10.4. Learning to Appreciate the Beauty in Diversity

Each culture can be seen as a kaleidoscope—a dynamic, multi-faceted tapestry of traditions, customs, languages, and values. Cultural understanding goes beyond simple tolerance; it involves appreciating and cherishing the geodesic diversity of cultures.

Education plays a crucial role in promoting cultural understanding. The right information can eradicate ignorance and help dissolve preconceived notions that breed misunderstandings. Learning about different cultures, their history, norms, values, and contributions to the world is a great starting point.

10.5. Bridging the Cultural Divide: Towards Global Solidarity

One of the most effective ways to spark worldwide unity and dialogue is strength in diversity. By focusing on our shared human experiences, we can bridge cultural divides and foster cross-cultural relationships.

Coming together in the face of adversity, learning from our mistakes, and reforming negative stereotypes can go a long way in shaping a future of global solidarity—a world where we aren't just a collection of rival cultures, but a tapestry of varied and cherished identities, bound together by shared experiences and mutual respect.

As we wrap up this chapter, let it be a gentle reminder that the journey toward cultural understanding is paved with kindness, empathy, and above all, respect for human diversity. This dialogue begins with acknowledging our cultural biases, keen listening, and refining our mental schemas towards the beauty that lies in our differences. Let us therefore carry this newfound understanding forward, as we strive to foster enduring connections that transcend borders and nurture the global village that is our shared home.

In building bridges over our cultural divides, remember: it's not about diluting differences, but about celebrating them. Because, in the end, our differences are what truly unite us, bringing colors that paint the vibrant tapestry of humanity. Welcome to the world stage, where every culture brings a unique performance, waiting for the audience to listen, understand, appreciate, and applaud.

Chapter 11. Brewing the Cultural Blend: Towards Unity in Diversity

In a world speckled with assorted cultures, understanding the blend of various traditions and practices becomes quite a fascinating journey. As we move through dimensions of different heritages, the complexities of this amalgamation translate into an enthralling exploration—a brewing pot of cultural unity in the heart of diversity.

11.1. The Intricate Threads of Cultural Fabric

Diverse cultures are like different threads—silently weaving around each other even in their solitary existence—to form a magnificent fabric. Each thread, symbolizing a unique culture, possesses its own charm that contributes to the splendor of the overall pattern. Their individuality in their unity paints a vibrant picture, a tableau of shared stories told worldwide.

11.2. Breaking the Ice: Barriers and Interfaces

Much like icebreakers in the Arctic ensuring clear passages, respectful curiosity serves a similar function when traversing cultural landscapes. Curiosity fuels learning, gradually melting away the barriers of stereotypes, biases, and misunderstandings. Humble inquiries about the traditions, history, and values of a culture hold the power to deepen our understanding and connect us closer to one another.

11.3. Unfolding the Bounties of Cultural Respect

No bounty is either too small or too grand in the pursuit of building bridges across cultural divides. Every attempt to learn a foreign phrase, every nod towards traditional dressing, or every gesture to honor native etiquette are remnants of the journey towards understanding. Such acts, when founded on respect and genuine curiosity, breed mutual understanding and evoke genuine gratitude.

11.4. Walking the Path of Diversity to Unity

The road from diversity to unity is a labyrinth of rich stories, shared histories, and mutual respect. It is laden with beautiful surprises and profound realizations about our shared human experience. Yet, navigating this maze could sometimes feel daunting. A compass may therefore be useful, not to point north, but to guide us towards the core of our shared humanity. This compass is opened through genuine conversations, shared meals, and shared spaces.

11.5. Preserving Individuality within Unity

While the goal is unity in diversity, let's not mistake it for creating a mono-cultural society. Cultures should coexist without losing their individuality and authenticity. Rather, it's the curiosity about these individual cultural manifestations that drives the process. This curiosity helps preserve and even celebrate individuality within unity.

11.6. Decoding the Language of Cultural Symbols

Symbols, rituals, and customs are languages in themselves—silently etching the memory of a culture's history. Decoding these symbols become portals to understanding long-preserved beliefs and practices. Consequently, when we appreciate and respect these, we partake in the heritage, inspiring a sense of belonging.

11.7. Tasting Unity in the Culinary Diversity

When we savor the myriad gastronomical journeys each culture invites us into, we do more than just tantalize our taste buds. We relish in the myriad stories, flavors, and sentiments these meals encapsulate. Cultural acceptance often begins with appreciating diversity on our plates before we embrace diversity within our hearts.

11.8. The Grand Tapestry: Reflective of Our Shared Values

Every culture, regardless of its distinctiveness, indicates shared values and common threads of humanity running through its tapestry. Identifying these shared values aids in establishing and refining our unified identity. Love, respect, kindness, honor, dignity—these universal principles form the underlying grid upon which every culture intricately weaves its unique patterns.

11.9. The Dance of Diversity: Art as a Medium

Art and culture are inseparable, mirroring each other in a beautiful dance. Art—a universal medium—expresses cultural emotions, histories, values, and narratives, serving as a golden bridge towards understanding other cultures. Through paintings, music, dance, and crafts, we can touch the soul of a culture, and in doing so, unite in a shared emotional understanding.

Through these explorations, what emerges is a world where unity does not mean unison but the coexistence of voices in a melodious symphony. From threads of a cultural fabric to a grand tapestry of shared values, every corner of this journey widens our perspective and enriches our understanding. As we continue to brew this cultural blend, it is vital to remember that unity in diversity is not an end, but a process—a process that derives strength from diversity and finds success in the everyday actions of people who dare to understand, appreciate, and celebrate the beautiful mix of cultures inhabiting our world—an exhilarating journey indeed!

www.ingramcontent.com/pod-product-compliance
Lightning Source LLC
Chambersburg PA
CBHW071012260726
48661CB00007B/2926